IF YOU BUILD IT, THEY WILL EXCEL

Leadership Principles for Building a Culture of Excellence in the Hospitality Industry

KHALID SHIEKH

NEWMAN SPRINGS PUBLISHING
320 Broad Street
Red Bank, NJ 07701

First originally published by Newman Springs Publishing 2023

ISBN 979-8-88763-120-2 (Paperback)
ISBN 979-8-88763-121-9 (Digital)

Printed in the United States of America

This book is dedicated to the great leaders and mentors I worked with over the past four decades.

Contents

Introduction

Great leaders have many remarkable qualities. They are visionary, creative, genuine, honest, passionate, empathetic, and inspirational people. They are also very thoughtful and persuasive. They are committed to their mission, objectives, and purpose in life. They possess admirable traits like foresight, integrity, stewardship, and passion for serving others. They are self-aware of their strengths and shortcomings. *They cultivate a passionate desire to succeed.*

Great leaders practice humility in their everyday interactions. They engage in empathetic listening and respond with sincerity and respect. They deal with people with integrity in their words and actions. They hold themselves accountable, acknowledge their failures, and diligently work to make things right. They inherently assume good intentions in others and help people in their endeavors. *In their personal and professional life, they continuously strive to learn and grow.*

Great leaders promote teamwork and positivity at the workplace. They build great teams. They build a culture of workplace excellence and lead with a passionate desire to succeed. They share their vision, strategy, plans, and purpose to achieve what is best for the organization. They get their teams involved in critical conversations and take everyone's input. They stay calm and keep the team moving forward. They know their people well and respect everyone they meet. They support their people and help them grow. They listen more and speak less. *Their behavior inspires their people.*

Great leaders come with different talents, backgrounds, and accomplishments. They are people too. They also have lived through life experiences just like any of us. They have a variety of behavioral styles and many noticeable strengths. Their styles often have been identified as authentic, influential, strategic, servant, focused or results oriented, etc. They also have some shortcomings and not-so-visible weaknesses. They are human but with an extraordinary talent and enormous passion for what they do. They inherently practice many motivational habits. Their inspirational passion and greatest desire to succeed are exemplary. Their emotional intelligence is admirable. They show a deep passion for their team's growth and help create more leaders. They want everyone around them to be at their best. *They have unique motivational abilities.*

In my experience, I have learned that there are two types of leaders: natural leaders and trained leaders.

Natural leaders have so many natural, pure, and likable qualities and traits. They are always full of joy, enthusiasm, creativity, and positivity. They generally possess a high degree of intelligence quotient and even a higher degree of emotional intelligence. When they speak, people listen. Their words always mean something. They are visionary, strategic, purposeful, and action-oriented. They want to accomplish the end in mind, through and with their people, and achieve greatness for the team. They also want to make the organization better. They attract smart and talented people on their team and help them further grow. They are committed to supporting their team and mentor their people. *They help create more leaders and always are on a mission.*

Trained leaders are very methodical, detail-oriented, and possess extraordinary technical knowledge. They always have objectives, goals, and strategies. They are thoughtful and also very action-oriented. They want to accomplish the end in mind through their people but by following plans, processes, procedures, and policies. They are always very engaged with their people and respectful in their interactions. They may or may not be as likable as the natural leaders but always deserve respect for their commitment, tenacity, and great intentions. They also want to make the organization better. They are hard workers and want the team to succeed as well. *They also help create more leaders and always have a plan.*

But the story does not just end there. They both achieve greater successes in their own way. They continue to grow and develop themselves. They learn new skills and have their own vision of becoming a more successful leader. They both strive to build great teams. They build a great workplace culture, help their people grow, and achieve pinnacles of success for the team, the organization, and themselves. *They both guide and mentor their people and help the organization become better and more successful.*

To highlight, the great leaders habitually:

- ➢ Do more and say less.
- ➢ Lead innovative initiatives hands on.
- ➢ Continuously learn new skills and develop new knowledge.
- ➢ Apply critical thinking in problem-solving.
- ➢ Acknowledge others' strengths and compliment sincerely.
- ➢ Speak what is true, kind, and necessary.
- ➢ Routinely show their gratitude, humility, and honor to others.
- ➢ Inspire others through their personal passion.
- ➢ Lead by example.
- ➢ Are guided by their intrinsic values and a greater good.
- ➢ Act in a thoughtful and purposeful manner.
- ➢ Envision, plan, and act with an end in mind.
- ➢ Behave in a caring, genuine, and authentic manner.
- ➢ Build meaningful and win-win relationships.
- ➢ Are passionate about earning their team's trust.
- ➢ Put their people first in almost all situations.
- ➢ Value, respect, and appreciate their team's achievements.
- ➢ Provide their team with clear and easy-to-follow directions.
- ➢ Invite their team's input and ideas on a regular basis.
- ➢ Ask others to speak their mind and listen with intent to learn.
- ➢ Work with diligence and tenacity to make things happen.
- ➢ Are generally very engaged, disciplined, and organized
- ➢ Balance their life with both intrinsic and extrinsic motivations.

> ➤ Deploy a high degree of energy for their endeavors.
> ➤ Support their team and are always willing to serve them.
> ➤ Seize every opportunity to celebrate their team's successes.
> ➤ Strive to live an inspiring and purposeful life.

Highlight the traits that you feel you practice in your leadership role today. Note to self which ones you would like to work on this month or this year.

I have served in leadership positions with two of the world's most successful hospitality services companies for more than thirty-six years. From corporate services district manager to healthcare support services multiple services' senior director in major medical centers around the country. In my fortunate journey from an assistant manager to an accomplished mid-level administrator, I earned several awards and recognitions, for which I am always proud of and grateful to my teams and the organizations.

I always felt that my most notable gain and honor was that I had the opportunity and fortune to work with some great, inspirational, and accomplished leaders in both health care and corporate services. I learned and retained so much from their great leadership skills and their everyday inspirational behaviors. I was always in awe of their accomplishments. I thought it would be fulfilling for me to share my firsthand experience, enhanced knowledge, and my personal passion for leadership by writing a book for other leaders in the hospitality industry.

If you are in a position of leading people in the hospitality industry, this book is for you. I am sharing the nine most effective principles that I learned from these leaders. I was so inspired that I dedicated myself to follow as best as I could. I recommend that you consider adopting these in your daily work life as well. Greater success and enormous personal fulfilment will follow equaling to your commitment, efforts, dedication, and passion for your personal growth and success. *You will make even a greater positive impact on your team and the organization. You can accomplish both your intrinsic and extrinsic motivations by following these principles.*

1

Begin with a Leader's Mindset

If your actions inspire others to dream more, learn more,
do more and become more, you are a leader.

—*John Quincy Adams, Sixth US President*

In the hospitality industry, people in leadership positions are called managers. Titles can range from regional manager to unit manager or department manager to assistant manager. Some businesses even assign such managerial titles to specific roles such as food production manager, customer service manager, or store manager. These managers are responsible to operate a business unit or a segment of a business. They are also accountable for achieving certain financial and operational objectives. These managers accomplish their preassigned goals through the hard work and dedication of their people. *These "people" are their most valuable asset.*

Today, this asset is being developed by the "managers." The world of leadership is evolving! The future of leadership is more inclusive, caring, empowering, authentic, purposeful, and rewarding! How are these managers positioned for success in this endeavor?

Tomorrow they will be led by the *"leaders"* instead of the managers! Together they will achieve more, grow more, and accomplish more for both the people and the organization! Their work life will

1

be more productive, enjoyable, meaningful, admirable, inspirational, and rewarding!

Today, if you are able to manage a business through your people, you are in a leadership position. You will need to practice great leadership principles to achieve much more than just your goals and objectives. *You will need to change your paradigm on how you do your job and interact with people! You will rethink how you coach, lead, and help your team grow! You will learn how to take thoughtful actions and become more of an authentic, caring, inclusive, compassionate, accomplished, and inspirational leader. Putting that altogether, you will become a great leader of tomorrow!*

> *Management is about arranging and telling.*
> *Leadership is about nurturing and enhancing.*
>
> —*Tom Peters, American Author*

Managers manage people to achieve preassigned goals, and things generally remain the same. Leaders lead people and help them and the organization grow, prosper, and become better. In my long career, whenever I was interviewing for a higher position, I prepared myself by learning all the details about that position. Additionally, I was always prepared to share with the interviewers how and what I was going to do to improve the organization. I would also share how closely I work with the people and dedicate myself to building great teams, how I would lead our team to achieve organization's objectives but also how they will personally benefit and grow from it. Whenever I was asked how will I manage their business, my response always was, "*I am not here to manage your business, I am here to make it better!*"

> *The manager accepts the status quo, the leader challenges it.*
>
> —*Warren Bennis, American Scholar*

Leaders' mindsets are what guides them every day. Their every word and action are geared toward their people, passion, and purpose. When you are leading a team of people, you need to have a vision, strategy, plan, and purpose. If you want to make a significant positive impact on your team and the organization, you need to carry a people-centered mindset and a mission that directs and guides you to:

- ➤ Be an empathetic listener.
- ○ Respond with sincerity and compassion.
- ➤ Get to know your people.
- ○ Their likes, dislikes, their goals, dreams, and challenges.
- ➤ Earn their respect.
- ○ Show respect first in your manners and interactions.
- ➤ Build trust with your people.
- ○ Practice integrity in everything you do or say.
- ➤ Speak less and listen more.
- ○ People want you to understand them.
- ➤ Build meaningful professional relationships.
- ○ Know and help them achieve their goals.
- ➤ Support their development.
- ○ Assist with professional growth opportunities.
- ➤ Become an engaged mentor.
- ○ Coach and guide their development.
- ➤ Show respect to every one you meet.
- ○ Make eye contact, smile, and remember their name.
- ➤ Share with your team your purpose in life.
- ○ This helps them respect and support you.
- ➤ Share your creative side.
- ○ It excites your people.
- ➤ Be genuine and authentic.
- ○ Smile and be truthful.
- ➤ Be trustworthy.
- ○ Say and do what is right and when it is right.
- ➤ Share your story to gain trust.
- ○ People want to know you.
- ➤ Model motivational behavior.

- ○ Help and show kindness.
- ➢ Be a little vulnerable.
- ○ Let them see a human in you.
- ➢ Be self-aware.
- ○ Balance your emotional intelligence to the situation.
- ➢ Empower people.
- ○ Let your people try new and unique endeavors.
- ➢ Get people involved in the thought process.
- ○ It helps them feel inclusive.
- ➢ Stay focused on the mission.
- ○ Your people will support you.
- ➢ Acknowledge your people's strengths.
- ○ Admire their strong traits in a meaningful manner.
- ➢ Make people feel great about themselves.
- ○ They will remember it for a lifetime.

In a leadership position, no matter how large or small of a team you may be leading, following these behaviors can bring you much personal fulfillment and greater success for your team and the organization. People on your team will feel respected, honored, and glad to be part of the mission and purpose and the organization. It will also bring greater honor, personal growth, and inner satisfaction to them. Your new mindset will motivate people in your team to also want to become a leader of tomorrow! It will also be a great inner fulfillment for you to help create more leaders and make many more lives better!

You manage things; you lead people.

—Grace Murray Hopper, American Computer Scientist

Questions to ponder about your everyday interactions with the people who are around you at work:

1. Do they trust you?
2. Do they respect you?
3. Do they follow you?

4. Do they listen when you speak?
5. Do they support you?
6. Do they know you?
7. Do they like you?

If the answer to any of these pondering questions is a no, the leader needs to rethink and bring a positive change to their mindset first!

2

Put People First and Serve Their Needs

Leadership is all about people. It is not about organizations. It is not about plans. It is not about strategies. It is all about people motivating people to get the job done. You have to be people centered.

—*General Colin Powell*

Your people want to be valued and respected

Your people will provide exceptional service to your customers if they feel valued, well-respected, and are well-trained. They expect their leader to be a great listener, compassionate, trustworthy, and sincere. Your people deserve your empathy and appreciation! They also want your support for their ongoing personal growth and development. Such actions on your part will inspire them to follow you and help you achieve pinnacles of success for the organization.

In 1977, I was working for a restaurant company as a manager in the Chicago area. We had a new district manager come onboard, replacing a very kind and engaged leader. Right from the beginning, many of us managers noticed his controlling actions. In his office, behind the desk, there was a huge poster on the wall depicting a lion in the jungle with the caption "Here, Lion Is the King!" He crossed out the word *lion* and put his name instead. So the poster read, "Here, Joe (not his real name) Is the King." He believed in it and behaved in the same manner. Within six months, three of his top-performing managers, including me, left the company. A few months later, he got fired! *He had put himself first!*

Your people want integrity in your words and actions

People in your team expect and respect integrity and transparency in your words and actions. This must be an inherent quality and practiced as a habit and not as a job function. Being genuine and trustworthy creates enormous loyalty. People will listen and believe you, even when what you say is not in their personal best interest. They want to know the facts, the truth, and clarity. *A leader cannot let them down!*

A few years ago, as a senior general manager for support services at a major medical center, I had to reprimand an operations supervisor. I met with her in the presence of another female manager. My demeanor was respectful and kind. My words were compassionate and sincere. I presented only the facts as I knew them. After I concluded, I offered to listen to her side. She had tears in her eyes and stated that she had made a mistake and that she was disappointed in herself. I listened with empathy and respect. I comforted her and assured her that she was still the same great supervisor as always and that this episode was behind us. I thanked her for being honest and understanding of the purpose of the meeting! She was pleased and stated this was a "learning" moment for her, and that she plans to become as best of a supervisor as possible, for her team, going forward. *Over the next few months, I observed her continued progress and growth as a leader of her team, and I was grateful for this positive development.*

Your people will feel your emotional intelligence

Successful leaders know their personal values and recognize their strengths as well as their shortcomings. Their values and day-to-day behaviors are instilled in them through their life experiences. They also know how some of their behaviors may sometimes set the wrong tone for the team. So they practice self-control and make full efforts to improve and make a better leader of themselves along the way. They also develop a high degree of personal emotional intelligence. This helps them stay grounded and keep mindful of what their role is as a leader.

In our everyday business and personal life, occasionally, we are faced with a situation that may trigger some negative emotional response that may not quite be the response you would give if you can contain your emotions. The successful and emotionally intelligent leaders just walk away from such situations to stay above the fray, even though they feel righteous. *In the long run, they are much better off emotionally and earn respect of people around them.*

Your people want to be heard

People around you want you to talk less and listen more. Leaders with effective communication skills practice "seek to understand first before being understood" habit when interacting with anyone. They know how important it is to the speaker to be heard and understood. Great leaders give other people the freedom to share their ideas and concerns without any fear. They acknowledge and verify what was said and what they understood. Being a great listener is a leadership strength that helps other people to speak their mind. *It's not only a habit but also a virtue!*

Often people on your team may have ideas or a personal matter to share with you or seek advice. They must have confidence in your ability to listen with empathy and sincerity to understand what they have to say. At the conclusion, thoughtful leaders will summarize what was said and what is expected of them. In personal matters, when appropriate, they will sympathize and offer any assistance that may be helpful and acceptable. A follow-up and follow-through meeting is essential to close the matter. *This active and compassionate listening skill is admired by all team members and helps the team members build trust with the leader and loyalty to the organization.*

Your people want you to be passionate, humble, and inspirational

One of the intrinsic qualities great leaders possess is their passion for what they do. They enjoy making a difference in other people's lives. They enjoy reaching higher levels of success through hard work and diligence. They love building great teams. They find happiness and fulfillment in leading people to achieve what may have been deemed unreachable previously. They also realize that their words, habits, behaviors, and actions are a great example for the team to follow. Great leaders know that their people will follow if they are valued, appreciated, inspired, and growing. *Being humble and grateful to their people is an inherent quality they possess and are always prepared to serve their people's needs in any way they can.*

At a recent assignment as a consultant for environmental services in a major medical center, I came across many great people in our frontline staff. I noticed many great qualities these people exhibited and how diligent they were in their patient care duties. They were also helping each other and working as a team. This behavior was so astonishingly admirable, as it was during the pandemic and where additional work stress was also prevalent.

I was so impressed with specifically four people that I spoke with them individually, not just to compliment about their work ethics, but also to thank them for being such great people and the valued team members! *After my brief one-on-one meeting with them, I noticed that each of them had a great happy smile, as if I lit something deep inside them. They were inspired by my sincere and honest thoughts and the recognition of their hard work and their greatness as people! They each thanked me with a great smile and humility. I also observed that after this positive and complimentary encounter with me, they were more vibrant and cheerful, not just the rest of the day but also the rest of the week.*

Your people want you to serve their needs

Successful leaders understand the value of being a servant and helpful leader. They assume good intentions of their team members and respect their concerns about their immediate needs. Some of them may need new equipment or a specific training so they can perform their day-to-day job duties better. Some may have a family need to address and request you to consider their schedule change proposal. Some may need you to entertain some ideas on how they can work better as a team if some roles or processes were redesigned. They want to do their jobs better for the good of the team. They want you to be a steward of their development and continued growth. *They want to grow, and many of them aspire to become a leader like you. They want their needs served.*

One of my servant leaders' habits that benefitted me the most was a monthly formal meeting with a number of employees, one-on-one, to document their thoughts on a variety of mostly work-related matters. This formal discussion included gathering thoughts on their:

- ➢ Personal and their family's state of well-being.
- ➢ Ideas of improvements in their area of responsibility.
- ➢ Area's equipment needs or any existing equipment's repair issues.
- ➢ Desire for any specific personal training needs.
- ➢ Input on improving the organization.
- ➢ Desire and direction for their personal development.
- ➢ Compliment or special thanks for any team member's assistance or a specific accomplishment.

Once this interaction was documented, it became a part of their personal performance file. It also became my leadership responsibility to respond to and resolve what the employees' needs and recommendations were. Depending on the importance or urgency of the matter, I proceeded to accomplish what was reasonably expected of me. I kept the employee updated on a weekly basis. In our monthly team meetings, I would briefly update the entire staff of what I was working on. This was one of the best and the most effective ways for me to be of service to my team members individually as well as a team. And as a result of my response and actions, our team and the organization were becoming noticeably better. *This one habit of doing things for my team contributed significantly toward making me a more effective and respected leader!*

What you do has a far greater impact than what you say.

—*Steve Jobs, Apple Inc. Cofounder*

Questions to ponder about your everyday role as a leader for the people who are around you at work:

1. Do you value their contributions?
2. Do you show your respect to them?
3. Do you say what you mean?
4. Do you follow up and follow through?
5. Do you respond to and serve their needs?
6. Do you listen with the intent to understand?
7. Do you show your gratitude?

If the answer to any of these pondering questions is a no, the leader needs to intentionally put people first in their behavior! And if you answered yes, what can you do to enhance this action?

3

Share Your Vision, Strategy, Plan, and Purpose

*The very essence of leadership is that you have to have
a vision. You can't blow an uncertain trumpet.*

—*Theodore M. Hesburgh, President, University
of Notre Dame, 1952–1987*

Successful leaders have a clear vision, defined strategy, thoughtful plan, and specific goals for the organization. They also have a greater purpose in mind, not just for the organization but also for the personal growth of the team members and the broader community in which they live and serve. They aspire to make a positive difference in other people's lives. They empower others in pursuit of happiness and their inner fulfillment! Great leaders take responsibility for their position. They strive to impact positively the lives of people around them and those who are impacted by their decisions and actions. *They aim to make lives better for all!*

I worked at a major medical center as the director of support services for nearly five years, over fifteen years ago. This was probably the best job in my entire forty-plus-year career in the hospitality industry. I reported to a highly energetic, focused, talented, and accomplished administrator. I admired and respected his inherent strengths, personal compassion, emotional intelligence, empathetic listening skills, inspirational qualities, and passion for his team's continued development and growth. He was also focused on improving the organization operationally and its continued growth, both in the short- and the long-term. He had shared his vision, strategy, and plans with his immediate direct reports as well as his superiors. A number of the department directors that reported to him were his team. We were all very clear about his mission and a greater purpose.

As a team, we bought into it, and we all believed in it. We had to keep the people, patient, families, and the community on top of our minds in everything we did. We were to work together as a coherent and committed team. At the same time, we were to operate our departments in a financially prudent manner as well. He would personally lead many projects around the medical center and was very active and engaged in the decision-making processes. He trusted each of us to do our jobs optimally and helped the organization accomplish its goals and objectives. He also wanted each of us to continue to grow. He had integrity in his words and actions and was respectful to everyone he met. He was always appreciative of his team's successes and celebrated with them! *He was an inspirational leader!*

As a team, not only did we receive many recognitions for reaching or exceeding our operational goals consistently, but we also proudly served our community for the better. To me, he was an exemplary leader. He was the leader to follow and learn from and be continually inspired. Over the years, he received multiple promotions and became the CEO of the entire health system. He not only succeeded for himself, but also many of his team members had grown into higher positions! *As a leader, he helped develop more leaders and made many lives better, including mine!*

Hospitals around the country strive to provide excellent medical care to their patients every day. Their mission, objectives, and core values are all about patient's health and well-being! Their strategies and plans are directed toward achieving best possible health outcomes, and as a result, the highest patient satisfaction score. Each department and its staff are committed to enhancing patients' experiences and provide them comfort and care during their stay at the hospital. *Patients are their focus and at the heart of everything they do!*

Successful hospitality businesses, whether local and small or multinational and large, similarly strive on serving their customers with excellence and offering fine products. They are also focused on providing value to their customers for their dollars. They want to exceed their patrons' expectations and create an environment of repeat business. They want their brand to become dependable and trustworthy. They want to grow, expand, and achieve optimal financial results on an ongoing basis, as a result. *Highly satisfied and repeat customers are their focus in everything they do!*

The successful and accomplished leaders who lead major medical centers or a single department within a hospital or lead a multinational corporation or one of their smaller business segments have one common theme—they all share their vision, strategy, and plan with their teams and all of the people around them. They want their team's buy-in, dedication, and commitment to achieve the goals and objectives set forth by them. *They want to and always make things happen for the organization and the team. They also carry a greater purpose for the people they work with and the communities they serve! They always have a mission and are dedicated to live it!*

> *There are three types of people in this world: those who make things happen, those who watch things happen, and those who wonder what happened.*
>
> —*Mary Kay Ash, American Businesswoman*

Vision

A great leader's clear vision of success is always in line with the organization's mission and core values. This is an essential first step toward achieving success. It clarifies the future, sets forth the direction, and it motivates and excites the team. It provides guidance and rejuvenates energy at every step going forward. Vision is always strategic, inspirational, and specific in the organization's future direction. Additionally an effective vision is created toward a common goal to benefit both the end user and the organization. This ultimately benefits both in the near and the long terms. The end user may be a patient in a hospital, a retail customer in the hospitality industry, or any other paying entity. *The vision must be transforming, of growth and sustainable in nature, and based on integrity and trust.*

Strategy

Sharing their defined strategy is the leader's next logical step toward achieving the vision laid out by them. They also seek input and buy-in to their strategy. The next step requires assigning responsibilities, developing budgets, establishing timelines, and creating reasonable and achievable goals. To execute the strategy, the organization and the leaders must create talented and expert operational teams. They recruit extremely talented, highly accomplished, thoroughly experienced, and mindfully supportive people on their teams. They place the "right people" in the "right seats" and steer the bus going in the "right direction." They are not afraid to move people around in the proverbial bus, if necessary, to make the journey more successful. They also set clear expectations for the team. They commit to staying engaged for guidance and support as needed. They provide the team the resources and the staffing they need. These actions motivate highly energized teams of people to move the team and the organization forward in an efficient manner. This group of people work together as a collaborative force to help achieve the desired results. *Their expertise, dedication, and the strategic actions keep the organization moving forward and continuously accomplish desired results!*

Plan

Detailed and thoughtful planning, from the beginning to the end, is the next crucial step toward achieving desired results. The leaders share an overview of their plan. To work out the details, it takes an experienced team of people, including a thought leader, a diligent operational expert, and an accomplished organizational planner. They work together and create a feasible and easy-to-follow detailed plan. The details must align with the leader's vision and strategy and support the organization's mission and core values. This is as much of a managerial task as it is leadership work. The plan must be specific and focused on clearly defined timelines. The plan will be different for each organization based on their size and location. It will also be different for each service line or a business segment. The operational responsibilities for each service line will be assigned specifically to align with the team's expertise. It is absolutely imperative that the right people are assigned the right tasks at the planning stage to carry out their role in the plan. *As a result, the team will have a detailed and well-coordinated plan to follow.*

Purpose

Living a purposeful life is a belief that most accomplished leaders embrace. At work and in their daily life, they want to bring and add value to other people's lives. They do not want to just exist; they would rather be a positive force and have a mission to be helpful and nourishing to others. They see their world beyond their extrinsic achievements. They regularly volunteer their time and resources to various charities and noble causes in their communities. They endeavor to live a kind and meaningful life and encourage people around them to do the same. The impact they want to create on humanity is bigger than themselves. Their purpose may be driven by their religious beliefs and/or their life experiences. Regardless they are deeply committed to bringing a positive change to the people's lives, however and wherever they can. *By their everyday kind behavior and being humble and purposeful, they light a fire in others to do the same.*

In my more than thirty years' service in mid-level hospitality leadership positions, I am proud to share that each organization that I worked for and their top leaders were committed to serving their communities purposefully. A few examples of our volunteering and service to the communities were:

➢ Working hands on for the Habitat for Humanity projects.
➢ Celebrating annual cancer survivors in family picnic days.
➢ Celebrating annual International Nurses Day and their families picnic day.
➢ Setting up monthly nutritional education kiosk at the local community events.
➢ Supporting Cancer Awareness Month and fundraising drives.
➢ Participating in the National Heart Healthy fundraising drives.
➢ Participating in annual health fairs for the community with educational fun events.
➢ Participating in annual local parks/community centers cleanup day.
➢ Organizing and leading the annual promotion of Great American Smokeout day.
➢ Participating in the local United Way fundraising.
➢ Organizing Toys for Tots gifts collection at Christmas holidays.
➢ Participating in several community-based wellness awareness events.
➢ Leading a quarterly Five-Mile-a-Day Walkathon.

There were many more events that I participated in along with our leaders. *Such events brought our community an extraordinary service and a joy to all of us who volunteered.*

If you are a new leader

If you are a newly appointed leader or in a new role as the leader of an organization, you have much more work to do before you can share any of your vision, strategy, or plan. You will have to develop it first. You may have a foundational knowledge and relevant experience, but you still have to get to know the people and the place in great details before you proceed. *Remember, when you are "green," you are still growing!*
You will need to:

> - Learn the place, the people, and the current operational practices.
> - Assess the capabilities of your team, their strengths, weaknesses, and challenges.
> - Study the patients' and/or customers' existing satisfaction levels.
> - Build working relationships with other colleagues and key internal customers.
> - Learn existing operational systems and processes.
> - Evaluate current financial feasibility and possible future opportunities.
> - Understand each area's workflow and near-term capital needs.
> - Get key people involved in developing goals and objectives.
> - Get the team's input on their aspirations and ideas for improvements.
> - Think and rethink your strategy and plans before going any further.
> - Prepare mentally and emotionally to begin the leader's work.
> - Receive your team's buy-in on your vision, strategy, and plans.
> - Show and share your passion and love for what you plan to do.

The only way to do great work is to love what you do.

—Steve Jobs, Apple Inc. Cofounder

Questions to ponder about your engagement style with the people who are around you at work:

1. Do you routinely promote the organization's mission statement?
2. Do you inherently practice the organization's core values?
3. Do you formally share your vision, strategy, plan, and purpose?
4. Do you regularly update the progress being made?
5. Do you adjust your strategy and plan as needed?
6. Do you recognize and reward the contributions being made by your team?
7. Do you routinely ask for your team's continued support?

If the answer to any of these pondering questions is a no, the leader needs to rethink their promotional and influential skills! Reflect on what have you done today to engage with your team.

4

Focus On Employee Satisfaction and Their Development

Take care of associates and they will take care of the customers.

—Marriott International, Inc., One of their core values

Satisfied and inspired employees in the service industry who are genuinely respected, treated with compassion, well-compensated, properly trained, involved in decision-making processes, and are recognized and rewarded for their outstanding work are the heart of a successful organization. They will do everything possible to provide exceptional service to their customers or the people they serve on a consistent basis. They love what they do and are proud of it. It's called the service excellence culture! The end users may be patients in a hospital being served their meals or their rooms being cleaned, retail cafeteria customers, patrons in a restaurant, or any other service industry customers. These satisfied and inspired employees will support each other, be very productive, and excel at their tasks and duties. They follow the standards, go above and beyond their duties, immensely enjoy their day at work, and make the business or the facility run smoothly and efficiently. *These are happy and engaged employees!*

In 2006, I was the senior general manager for support services at a major medical center in Oklahoma City. The senior leadership had planned a major celebration for the hospital week. I was assigned to procure two hundred dozen of fresh-baked cookies from a local bakery. I was advised that there were a few places I could reach out to, to get quotes and the assurance that the product will be of superb quality at a reasonable price and delivered safely and on time. I called a well-established cookie company store at a local mall to speak with the manager to get some ideas and a quote. A very enthusiastic and vibrant voice answered the phone with an appropriate and cheerful greeting. That was my first positive impression of this place. I asked to speak with the manager. She very politely replied, "The manager is not in right now, but I will gladly assist you in her absence. How may I help you?"

I could hear her smile, feel her enthusiasm, and visualize her engaging style in her voice. She was committed to helping a potential customer over the phone. This was the second positive impression of this place. I described the reason I was calling, and she responded, "We would be honored to prepare two hundred dozen cookies for the hospital staff. We are very experienced at preparing large quantities, so please give us the opportunity."

Of course, that statement sealed the deal for me. I did not even ask the price. She set up a time for me to come meet with her and the manager the next day to plan out the variety, price, and the delivery times, etc. I was thoroughly impressed with her salesmanship, happy voice, enthusiasm, and engaging style over the phone.

The next day, when I met with the manager and her, we quickly finalized the arrangement for the cookies order and the price, etc. Before I left the store, I asked her what makes her so happy, cheerful, energetic, engaging, and customer-focused. She replied in three words, "It's our culture!" *Our manager treats us with respect, dignity, fairness, and appreciation every day, and we treat every customer the same way!*

It takes a dedicated and committed leader who creates an employee-focused culture and places employees first in almost all situations! They build a service excellence culture where both the end users and the employees benefit tremendously. As part of their day-to-day work and behavior, committed leaders follow six leadership strategies and employee engagement principles. These are:

1. *Recruiting the best*

The right people for the right jobs! Recruiting or hiring the very best people for any job in the organization is the foundation of building a great service excellence culture. It starts with the position posting. The first sentence of the job requirement must state clearly about the service excellence culture and the importance of the newly hired people's individual role in enhancing it. In a live (or virtual) interview, it must be reemphasized that if hired, they are expected to make a positive difference in the prevailing culture of the organization or the department.

Hiring for the technical skills is important but not as significant as a candidate's personal presentation skills. The interviewer should intentionally look for the candidate's personal grooming, greeting style, appropriate eye contact, politeness in their demeanor, and a pleasant smile. During the interview process, if they are paying attention to their personal presentation details, they are very likely to pay attention to following your service excellence standards while at work. Technical skills can be improved by further training, once the candidate is onboard. But the personal presentation skills and the attention to details habits are rarely improved!

Many organizations utilize a predesigned interview format with specific questions. Some other leaders utilize their own format designed specifically to a position and its role's requirements. No matter what format is being utilized for the basic interview questions, the leader must also look for the following three traits by simply asking some probing questions to their answers:

1. *Integrity in their answers.*
2. *Intelligence in their thinking.*
3. *Interactive skills and their body language.*

What you see and feel about the candidate's presentation in an interview is likely what your patients or customers will experience behind your back. This is also what the other employees in the department will encounter when the candidate is hired. Some organizations also conduct peer interviews, which can be beneficial from a team-building stand-point. But the leader must make the final decision in the selection of the new hire!

2. *Elevating the compensation*

Employees want to be paid well! In today's economy, compensation matters more than some organizations believe. We are in a post-pandemic, competitive service economy, more so than perhaps ever before. There is competition out there for the most desirable service-level talent. To attract great people, the compensation must be above the marketplace threshold. This is a challenge that support services' department directors in many hospitals and many leaders in other service industry businesses face every day. Even though they want to recruit great people, the salary scales often do not meet the candidates' expectations. Successful leaders are finding ways to convince higher-ups in the organization to elevate the pay structure so the excellent candidates can be attracted to join the team. The benefits package being offered may attract some desirable candidates, but most want a higher base pay. *They know their value and are looking to be compensated relative to their talent, skills, and abilities.*

3. *Providing tools and training*

Employees want to do a great job! A leader must begin with this premise and presume good intentions in others. Employees cannot perform at their best if they do not have the right tools they need or the tools they work with are not in optimal condition. The organization must also have a clearly defined training program. An initial formal training period of five to ten days for every new hire for their position is essential. The training or orientation manager's knowledge, behavior, attitude, and enthusiasm will create the first impression on the new team member. If the new hire's training module also includes shadowing a "lead" employee, this leader must exhibit the culture that the interviewer outlined earlier during the interview process. Ongoing monthly and/or quarterly training and refresher sessions for each position must also be conducted. A leader should conduct monthly rounding with the new employees to make sure that they are satisfied with their job tasks, tools, training, and the environment. A leader should take action when the employees' needs have changed. A leader cannot lose an employee's dedication, energy, positive mindset, and interest by not providing them with what they need to perform at their best!

4. *Practicing employee involvement*

Employees have ideas! They want to do a great job, make a positive difference, and further improve the way they work. They want to accomplish more, be more efficient, and become more productive. A leader must listen to and get employees involved in both formal and informal fashions. The employees know their customers, the product, and are committed to providing service excellence. The leader must pay attention to and respect each employees' input. The most effective ways to get employees involved are:

1. By monthly rounding with a few employees in a formal manner.
2. Responding to their ideas in a formal manner within a reasonable time.
3. When planning a major operational change or introducing a new concept.
4. Before making any changes to an existing process or products.
5. Inviting some employees in brainstorming on problem resolutions.
6. By challenging them for further creativity and innovation in the department.

7. Keeping the door open for one-on-one meetings to listen to their thoughts or concerns.

5. *Integrating recognition and rewards as part of the culture*

Employees want to be appreciated! While employees enjoy an instant and sincere "Thank you" gesture by their leader, they also like and enjoy a formal reward and recognition program. Even though many organizations including most hospitals and other businesses in service industry have such programs, the employees prefer a department-level program as well. They also want to be recognized among their peers. Recognition and rewards program should have characteristics of both material and emotional rewards and recognition. Such a program should have the following components:

1. Be simple, fun, ongoing, and easy to follow.
2. It should include a handing of a card, a star, or an app-based points system for an instant gratification.
3. Cards, stars, or app-based points should have some redeemable value within the department or the organization.
4. The awardees should also be recognized in front of their peers and/or customers.
5. It should also include some monthly gifts giveaways, drawings, etc.
6. A quarterly and/or an annual celebration in the department or organization.
7. It should include an occasional handwritten "Thank you" note in the mail to acknowledge any special contribution.

6. *Supporting growth opportunities*

Employees want to grow! Well, most, if not all. It is the leader's responsibility to know and learn who wants to grow and in what fashion. Some would want to learn other duties and other areas within the department or the organization. Others may want to stay in their current area but would like to learn more and perhaps go for additional education, formal training, or vocational certification. Some may want to go for the next position up. Many organizations also have a tuition assistance program if the employee wants to get further education in their field or any other field of their personal interest and future growth. Here is how this works the best:

1. Leaders should ask the employees in their annual reviews about their personal vision of growth and development.
2. Offer candid and sincere advice and/or encouragement.
3. Give their recommendations to employees for the next steps.
4. Offer reasonable assistance, coaching, and mentoring when needed.
5. Seek human resources assistance when needed.
6. Document all conversations or related events.
7. Continue to support the employee throughout this long mentoring and developmental process.

The six strategies and principles noted above will help create an environment of highly satisfied employees and begin creating a service excellence culture. This is possible in any organization where the leader is committed, compassionate, and capable of envisioning and delivering on basic and simple strategies outlined above! Putting employees first in the hospitality industry is not a new concept. Making it happen takes a lot of effort and dedication by the leader. Rewards for the organization in return are enormous! The patients or the customers who experience exceptional service from your staff will let you and many others know, usually in a very big manner! That makes it so worthwhile.

Questions to ponder about your focus on your employees' satisfaction and growth:

1. Do you know every employee's name?
2. Do you greet every employee every day?
3. Do you round with the new hires daily?

4. Do you know if any employee needs new equipment, tools, or training?
5. Do you take your employees' inputs routinely?
6. Do you have a formal reward and recognition program?
7. Do you offer growth opportunities to the employees who want it?

If the answer to any of these pondering questions is a no, the leader needs to develop an action plan to build a team of satisfied employees!

5

Create a Workplace Excellence Culture

*Leadership should be more participative than
directive, more enabling than performing.*

—*Mary D. Poole, American Author*

I n healthcare support services, people not only serve other people,
but they also provide comfort, care, a helping hand, and a safe
environment! Whether they are serving patients with their meal,
cleaning their room, transporting them from their hospital room to
the lab and back, they are serving people! These people are also their
patients! These patients in a hospital are likely under the best possible
medical care of the hospital's very caring medical staff. They are also
in the hands of the most compassionate and comforting support services employees. These employees are carefully recruited because of
their service attitude, pleasant manners, and inherent people skills.
They are also very well-trained.

In the hospitality and service industry, in general, people serve
other people. In almost all cases, there is a human-to-human live
interaction. In the restaurant business, for example, this interaction
between the wait staff and the paying guest may repeat several times
during a meal service encounter. The guests may be a family having a
dinner for a special occasion or a group of business associates having
a lunch meeting. There are many scenarios in the business world

where people are serving other people and making a reasonable living doing so. They are also creating and leaving impressions with other humans in each interaction.

Serving other people, whether in a hospital or a restaurant or in any other service-oriented profession, is not for everyone. It takes a unique person with a special talent, positive service attitude, compassion, pleasant manners, and a lot of patience to thrive in this profession. It also requires a higher emotional intelligence to be very successful. Serving other people can also be very stressful for some people, at times. So, in this profession, the employees are carefully selected with that criterion in mind and are also very well-trained in their tasks and duties. *And when they excel at what they do, their patients, guests, and patrons will see it, feel it, and share their experience with everyone they know!*

To excel at providing exceptional service, the employees must first experience respect, compassion, sincerity, appreciation, and feel valued by their leader and the organization. They want to be properly compensated and given opportunities for further growth. They expect their leader to provide a clear direction, clarify expectations, and engage with them on a regular basis. They want all work-related issues to be resolved promptly and fairly. They also expect their leader to follow-up and follow-through on their words in a timely manner! These are the behaviors they want to experience from their leader at their workplace. *This is what makes the employees help shine brightly at what they do! It takes a thoughtful, dedicated, committed, creative, engaged, and supportive leader to build a great workplace excellence culture.*

In the previous chapters, I have discussed the importance of several leadership traits and principles that great leaders inherently practice as a habit and do so every day. These include:

- ➢ Carrying a leader's mindset.
- ➢ Putting people first and serving their needs.
- ➢ Sharing their vision, strategy, plan, and purpose.
- ➢ Focusing on employee satisfaction and their development.

To build a great culture of workplace excellence, the leader must also practice the following seven additional high impact traits and principles:

1. *Paint a clear picture and clarify expectations*

Employees want to know what is expected of them! Organized and disciplined leaders know that ambiguity slows down employees' drive and tampers their enthusiasm. The clearer the direction, the better the results. Most employees will go to tremendous lengths to achieve what the leader wants. They may even design their own path to achieve results if a clear picture has been painted toward the end in mind. They want to be fully onboard with the "plan" and get to work.

To accomplish any great task or achieve highly desired results from any team, a leader's effective communication skills also play an important role. They keep the directions simple and straightforward and present in an easy-to-follow manner. To avoid confusion, they verify that the employees understand their expectations and that the outcome is clearly defined. This leadership skill is always admired by the team and is essential for high team output!

2. *Make employees feel welcomed and appreciated*

Employees should look forward to their day at work! Compassionate and engaged leaders know that the employees enjoy being welcomed to their workplace. It takes a sincere greeting with pleasant smile and a polite eye contact to welcome each employee at the beginning of their day. Newly hired employees should be introduced to the entire team by the department or the organization's leader personally. Taking this new employee through the department and introducing one-on-one to their newest team member solidifies not only the new team member's confidence but also gives the existing team an engagement reinforcement! This one simple leadership behavior shows enormous respect and a great welcoming gesture to the new team member.

Employees appreciate an instant and sincere "Thank you" by their leader. Employees' individual and team's collective accomplishments should be highlighted in department meetings. They can also be recognized on the hospital or the organization's website. Any gesture of true gratitude toward the employees has an enormous boost to their morale. These leadership behaviors recharge employees' energy and enthusiasm!

3. *Treat employees fairly and with respect*

Employees can sense micro-inequities! Fair-minded and sincere leaders are aware of their everyday behavioral style when interacting with employees. They know that each employee is a unique person and has a certain special talent. They also learn what each employees' strengths and opportunities for growth are. They sense that employees are not necessarily looking for "equal" treatment, rather an equitable, just, and fair treatment.

With such awareness, these leaders purposefully and inherently show respect and kindness to each employee. They also encourage employees to speak with them if any one feels that they have somehow been ignored or slighted in any fashion. Such open-door communication is very effective in building mutual trust between the two. This leadership practice builds a long-standing mutual respect and an ongoing employees' commitment and dedication!

4. *Resolve issues promptly and fairly*

Employees want issues resolved! Practical and active leaders know how important it is to the employees that all work-related issues are addressed fairly and promptly. Even if the leader considers the matter to be minor, it should receive appropriate and timely attention. At times, disagreement between any two team members can occur. It is the leader's responsibility to immediately handle the situation and seek human resources assistance only if needed. Issues, when not addressed in a timely manner, can get escalated and may require more time and resources to resolve.

Leaders should work directly with the employees to find resolutions and common ground. Once a matter has been resolved, leaders must follow-up and follow-through with the employees to verify that the resolution outcome was to their satisfaction. This leadership practice builds employees' faith and trust with the organization and further improves their work environment.

5. *Have integrity in your words and actions*

Employees will be the first to trust you! Leaders with integrity know that they provide moral leadership with their words and actions every day. When a leader fails to deliver on their words, promises, or commitments, it will let employees down. It can also damage the trust and working relationship. Here are some basic and simple rules to follow to avoid such failures:

> ➢ Promise less, deliver more, when possible.
> ➢ Keep commitments simple and doable.
> ➢ Be aware of and avoid micro-inequities.
> ➢ Be loyal to your team and stay aware of their needs.
> ➢ Deliver bad news with empathy and compassion.
> ➢ Dignify employees' genuine disappointment.
> ➢ Apologize sincerely when needed.

At times a leader will make an honest mistake or a human error that impacts employees adversely in some fashion. When this happens, a genuine leader must be forthright, take responsibility, apologize, and correct the situation. This leadership practice will not only teach them a lesson but also build even stronger trust and bond with the employees.

6. *Hold self and team accountable*

Employees expect team and leadership accountability! Accomplished and thoughtful leaders practice self-accountability before they hold their team accountable. In a culture of workplace excellence, employees put forth the full effort every day. They are focused and committed to serving their patients, customers, and patrons above and beyond expectations. Nothing will slow them down until they sense a lack of consistent accountability of every team member.

All employees and leaders must follow the same set of rules and standards. When one team member fails to comply, standard counseling process needs to be followed. Most employees will respond to a direct, fair, and constructive approach. A written and formal developmental plan may also be needed in certain cases, as a last resort. When leaders hold themselves accountable in a meaningful manner, it creates a powerful and inspirational environment for the employees. This habit of self-accountability can motivate employees to feel great about their leader and the organization.

7. *Celebrate successes*

Employees love to celebrate successes! Fun-loving and grateful leaders seize on every opportunity to thank their teams, show their gratitude, and celebrate their successes! They know the positive impact of formally recognizing their team's achievements. Celebrations should be both in the form of preplanned activities and some spontaneous fun events. Here are a few suggestions:

> ➢ Annual departmental national recognition weeks.
> ➢ Let employees participate in planning such events.
> ➢ Hospital leadership should also be invited to thank the team.
> ➢ Recognition of star performances in monthly department meetings.
> ➢ A program where employees nominate fellow team members for recognition.
> ➢ Ongoing celebration for employees who receive customers' compliments.
> ➢ Department-wide monthly employees' birthday events.
> ➢ Any other creative events highlighting team's high performance.

> ➤ Foods and giveaways are always appreciated in all celebration events.

A workplace excellence culture is possible in any organization where a leader is committed, compassionate, respectful, and grateful to employees for their contributions. In addition to the leader being visionary, they must also communicate effectively. The leadership traits listed above can help leaders in creating a great workplace culture, a culture where the employees excel at what they do and deliver exceptional service to the people they serve, achieve their higher satisfaction and greater personal job satisfaction!

Questions to ponder about your efforts on building a workplace excellence culture:

1. Are you and your employees able to recite the organization's mission statement?
2. Do you hold monthly employee meetings to update on mission and objectives?
3. Do you celebrate and welcome new employees to your team?
4. Do you make the employees feel welcomed routinely in a professional manner?
5. Do you resolve issues promptly and fairly?
6. Do you hold yourself and the team accountable?
7. Do you celebrate successes of the individuals as well as the organization?

If the answer to any of these pondering questions is a no, the leader should prioritize and implement these actions to improve the workplace culture!

6

Build Great Teams and Make Organizations Better

Coming together is a beginning, staying together is progress, and working together is success.

—*Henry Ford, American Industrialist*

Teamwork is when a group of people or components work together in harmony to achieve a preplanned objective or a predesigned outcome. Having a clear understanding of the team's objectives and predefined goals and knowing everyone's role is very important. It provides the team members an opportunity to collaborate with and support each other. Each member can exhibit their strengths while simultaneously learning from each other. It is so valuable when you acknowledge other team members' strengths and compliment them with sincerity and admiration. It is equally valuable that when you receive compliments from the other team members that you stay humble and be appreciative of their kind gesture.

Building great teams is hard but very satisfying and rewarding work. It takes an experienced and thoughtful leader with an enormous foresight to build a cohesive and talented team. It takes even more energy and planning to design everyone's roles and responsibilities. Getting everyone to work together, like a well-coordinated team, can sometimes be challenging. It takes all team members with different roles and responsibilities to perform cohesively and optimally to achieve the team's mission and objectives. It takes everyone to do their part to do what is needed to be done. It takes a dedicated spirit of commitment, focused concentration, and a genuine desire to truly support and respect each other to become a great team.

Successful leaders look for talented, experienced, dedicated, and diligent people on their teams. Team members' strengths must match the requirements of the role they will play. Leaders also look for other admirable traits such as integrity, likability, respectful behavior, passion, supportive attitude, and effective communication skills.

Of all the things I have done, the most vital is coordinating those who work with me and aiming their efforts at a certain goal.

—*Walt Disney, Founder of The Walt Disney Company*

Imagine a scenario. It's midmorning and lunchtime is approaching. A patient in a hospital bed is feeling hungry. He reaches over to the bedside table and grabs his copy of the patient's room service menu. On the cover, there are some very appetizing and colorful food pictures. Just by looking at these pictures, he is anticipating a nice lunch tray with delicious food items prepared just for him. He is imagining what hot and cold food choices he would like to have. After all, he was not allowed to eat or drink any food or beverage by mouth all morning.

Then there is a gentle knock on the door, and his nurse enters the room smilingly and tells him that the doctor has cleared him for the lunch meal. He is elated to hear that and thanks her for the great news. Of course, his next question is, "How is the food here?"

She replies with a pleasant voice and full assurance that "our food service department is the best, and the food here is great!" She asks him if he has any questions about the menu or needs help in placing his order. He is pleased with the nurse's kind gesture of help! He tells her that he will call for his meal order a bit later when he is ready.

A few minutes later, the patient calls the room service order line, and a very friendly, pleasant, and courteous representative answers the phone. The interaction between the two about his food choices is very detailed and in line with the patient's diet guidelines. The representative helps him design a great meal tray to his liking. The patient is very satisfied with the courtesy and help he received from the room service representative over the phone. He is anticipating a great meal to arrive at the time that he wanted for the tray to be delivered.

There is a gentle knock on the door at about the time he is expecting his meal tray to arrive. A very pleasant and courteous room service hostess enters the room and introduces herself. She has his meal tray. She verifies that this is the right tray for this patient and places his meal tray in front of him on the overbed table. She requests that he verifies if the meal tray is accurate and appealing to him. He verifies that the tray is accurate and says that the food presentation looks very appetizing. She offers to come back in five minutes to see if he needed anything else. He is very impressed with the courtesy and politeness of the hostess who just served him his meal tray. A few minutes later, when the hostess comes back to check on him, he tells her that the food is great, and he is really enjoying it! He thanks her for checking back on him!

In the scenario described above, the patient experiences very professional, helpful, polite, and courteous service throughout. He also enjoys a great, freshly prepared, and delicious meal of his choice. *This excellent experience is made possible by the teamwork of many talented and dedicated people in the food and nutrition services department. His experience is further enhanced by the support and kindness of his nurse. I call this whole patient experience teamwork, and it's what's for lunch!*

It takes each of the following team of people to provide an excellent dining experience to every patient at every meal period, every day:

➤ The nurse offers to help and talks up to the food service department.

- The team that created the colorful and attractive room service menu.
- The room service representative helps each patient with service attitude.
- The tray line staff assemble the tray with care and accuracy.
- The team of cooks prepare fresh and appetizing hot foods.
- The team of prep cooks prepare fresh and appealing cold foods.
- The expediter verifies the tray presentation and the accuracy of the tray.
- The hostess is polite, courteous, and helpful when serving the tray.
- The dietitian designs the menu choices in line with the dietary guidelines.
- The executive chef leads the entire culinary team and assures high quality and recipe compliance.
- The patient services manager supports everyone on this team.
- The production manager orders the best possible food supplies.
- The dish room staff follow sanitary standards for cleaning dishes and utensils.
- The department director keeps the team motivated and inspired.
- The hospital's administrators support and appreciate the team.

Similarly, in other hospitality and/or retail businesses, the guests are served in an excellent manner because of a large, diligent, and dedicated team's superb and well-coordinated work. Many different people on each team, performing different roles and tasks in a disciplined and organized manner, make certain that the paying guests are provided a fine product and an excellent service. Whenever and wherever these customers experience a great team's work of excellence, they keep coming back. They also share their personal experiences with their own family and friends. This word of mouth helps the business thrive and further grow!

These teams of people work together toward a common goal to make the organization better. They are extremely talented in their profession and highly skilled in their duties. They are very well-trained and perform their tasks with pride and humility. They have an inherent talent to do their job well and do it with care and compassion. They do everything that needs to be done to achieve the organization's goals and objectives. They are also making their organization better.

They also follow some basic and proven teamwork principles. They have developed the ability and mindset to work together. They are committed to serving and supporting each other. They want to provide the best possible meal service experience to each patient they serve. Similarly the retail teams aim to provide the most valuable service experience to their paying customers. They understand and believe in the virtues of becoming a superb and cohesive team to do their jobs optimally. They also like and respect each other.

Listed below are the nine most effective and simple teamwork principles that they practice for achieving their goals and attaining high personal job satisfaction.

1. *Know your team's goals, objectives, and plans*

It is imperative that each team member understands clearly what the team's specific goals, objectives, and plans are. The more detailed the plan, the better it is for perfect execution. They also need to believe in the mission, the strategies, and the leadership's ability to successfully lead and support the team. They adjust their plans, if necessary, to keep the end in mind and in sight.

2. *Understand and clarify your role*

Every team member should clearly know and understand exactly what their individual role is and how their work contributes to the team's success. If a member is not certain about their exact responsibilities, they seek clarification for everyone's benefit. The team leader should verify that each member understands their role thoroughly.

If any role needs adjusting to make the team more productive, the leader will make that happen by working with their people.

3. *Respect and honor others' role*

Every team member has an important role to play and make positive contributions toward achieving the team's goals. Everyone on the team must respect, honor, support, and acknowledge other members' roles, successes, and their contributions. Honoring each other's contributions enhances team spirit and builds greater mutual respect.

4. *Support and help others*

Supporting and helping each other builds great trust and respect for each other. There are times when a fellow team member falls behind or has too much on their plate. A helping hand from the fellow members is an admirable and worthy gesture. Not to mention, it ultimately helps the team achieve their desired outcomes for the patients, guests, and the customers.

5. *Communicate clearly*

It starts with the leader. Everyone on the team should be appropriately and, in a timely manner, kept informed. A variety of communication mediums should be utilized to inform, promote, and share progress and results. Team members should also communicate among themselves in a clear and precise manner. Verifying what someone said and what you understood is very important.

6. *Resolve differences fairly and promptly*

When people work together, there is always a possibility of disagreements. At times, such incidents can be potentially detrimental to the team chemistry and may hamper achieving desired outcomes. Such situations must be resolved fairly and promptly. This is important to not let this cause lack of mutual respect. Team members should attempt to resolve such issues among themselves first, if possible.

7. *Follow-up and follow-through*

Following up and following through on your commitments is an essential piece of the bigger picture of teamwork. Promising less and delivering more is also a good habit. If a team member is counting on you, you cannot let them down. If a patient-related issue or a dissatisfied patron's complaint has been handed off to you, resolve it to their full satisfaction and in an efficient and kind manner.

8. *Cultivate desire for success and talk up others*

Every great team has some natural leaders. They show their passion, commitment, enthusiasm, and desire for success through their words and actions every day. They encourage, motivate, support, compliment, and talk up others. They are eager to show genuine, sincere, and heartfelt gratefulness to their team. This is how they cultivate a desire for success and honor all team members.

9. *Acknowledge and celebrate accomplishments*

The grateful leaders celebrate team successes and accomplishments routinely. They never fail an opportunity to thank their team in a meaningful way. They also promote their team's accomplishments within the organization. Acknowledging each other's successes in a formal and authentic manner shows sincerity and gratitude, and it strengthens team chemistry.

Great teams accomplish great deeds. It takes superb teamwork among all employees of the department or the organization to create an exceptional experience for the patients or the paying customers. Working together, supporting, and respecting each other, giving due recognition, promoting others, cultivating desire for success, and being grateful to each other is what makes a team great! The more cohesive the team, the better it is for the organization and its reputation.

Teamwork is the ability to work together toward a common vision. The ability to direct individual accomplishments toward organizational objectives. It is the fuel that allows common people to attain uncommon results.

—Andrew Carnegie, American Industrialist

Questions to ponder about your efforts toward building a great team and making the organization better:

1. Do all team members know the organization's mission, goals, and objectives?
2. Do all team members know their individual role and understand the importance of it?
3. Do they respect and support each other?
4. Do you keep your communications simple and clear?
5. Do you help in resolving their differences, if needed?
6. Do you follow up and follow through in a timely manner?
7. Do you cultivate a desire for success and celebrate accomplishments?

If the answer to any of these pondering questions is a no, the leader needs to reset and implement actions to address these core team building fundamentals!

7

Communicate Effectively

It's not what you say, it's what people hear.

—*Dr. Frank Luntz, Author*

One of the most noticeable and admired abilities that great leaders possess is that they communicate so effectively. Whether in person speaking one-on-one, in a small group meeting, or making a presentation to a larger audience, they know how to get the message across in a simple and positive manner. They know exactly what to say, how to say it, and what the audience needs to retain. They believe it is their responsibility to articulate the message, convey it in such a manner that engages the listener, and that the message is received as intended. Some leaders have this ability naturally, while others develop this important skill over time.

Over thirty-five years ago, I, along with my then eight-year-old son, attended a basketball camp for the youth conducted by an NBA head coach in Dallas, Texas. I had never played the game, but one statement that this head coach made to the young kids has stayed with me for all these years. He said to the eight- and nine-year-old kids that "when you are passing the ball to your teammate, it is your responsibility to do so in such a manner that he gets the ball with ease and where you intended to throw. Otherwise the ball may get stolen by the opponent."

I thought this was a valuable teaching to the kids, even beyond the basketball court. What I gained from it was that when you are speaking to others, it is your responsibility to do so in such a manner that the listener or the audience receives the message with ease and as you had intended. *Otherwise, the message may get lost or misunderstood.*

Anyone can learn and achieve this leadership strength if they follow some simple and basic principles for improving this skill. In this chapter, I am going to share some of the basic principles that I have seen great leaders follow. They excel in both *interpersonal skills as well as group presentation skills.* These simple principles, if followed, can help further improve your communication skills and make you an effective and positive communicator.

Positive Interpersonal Skills

When people talk, listen completely. Most people never listen.

—*Ernest Hemingway, American Novelist*

1. *Be an active listener*

Positive interpersonal communication begins with being an active and empathetic listener. Your eyes, ears, and mind must be engaged with the speaker. It takes a sincere effort to fully comprehend what message the speaker is trying to send. You may not fully comprehend if you do not pay full attention. In addition to their words, you must also observe their body language, sense their tone, and capture their emotions. Different people communicate differently, but they do show their true feelings, along with their words, in a noticeable manner. An engaged and active listener comprehends the words, senses the emotion, and retains the speaker's intent.

2. *Be interactive*

Any meaningful and positive dialogue requires two or more engaged and empathetic listeners rather than talkers. Instead of preparing your response to the words you hear, you should wait for the speaker to give you an opportunity to respond. It is important to repeat back and clarify what you heard and understood. This will alleviate any ambiguity. While speaking to others, smile politely and address them by their preferred name. It shows enormous respect. At times, it may require some patience on your part because the speaker may have a unique communication style or is overwhelmed with stress or emotions.

3. *Be sincere and authentic*

The act of sincerity in both listening and speaking situations makes any conversation a positive communication. People will notice your engagement style, authenticity, and level of sincerity almost immediately. There may be some situations during the conversation where it may become necessary for you to share your true feelings as well, but do so in a kind, gentle, and respectful manner. Be aware of your own facial expressions, hand gestures, and other body movements, which may be perceived as insincere or offensive. A pleasant smile on your face will make the listener comfortable in carrying on the conversation.

4. *Speak clearly*

Skillful interpersonal communication requires that you speak clearly and in a pleasant tone of voice. You should articulate words that are appropriate and easy to understand. The unclear speech shows a lack of articulation and risks losing the listener's interest. A monotone voice with no change in pitch or volume shows no emotion and is boring to the listener. Speaking too fast or too slow may irritate the listener and they may not hear or understand what you had to say. You should also observe how your words and emotions are being received by the listener. Make appropriate changes in your words, tone, pace, and emotions.

5.   *Show your gratitude*

People in their day-to-day business life and even in their personal life are often short of time. Sometimes they are low on energy or have a lack of interest in having a conversation with you. When people give you time and attention, they are really giving you a gift out of their life. That amount of time will never comeback for them! It is so important that you thank them for their time in having a conversation with you. Showing your sincerity and gratitude for their time makes them respect you. If the conversation benefitted you in a material sense, a follow-up with a written "Thank you" note may be appropriate.

Effective Group Presentation Skills

The single biggest problem in communication is the illusion that it has taken place.

—*George Bernard Shaw, Irish Playwright*

1.   *Prepare and practice*

For many people, speaking to a group is the greatest fear in their lives. Just the thought of facing strangers in the audience makes them nervous and even lose some sleep over it. But this fear is often exaggerated in their minds. To ease this common fear, first begin preparing ideas and concept for the presentation in your mind. Conduct proper research that may be required. Once you are comfortable with the thoughts and the information gathered, put it all on paper and create a rough draft. Read several times to edit or make changes where needed. Once the presentation is finalized, practice perfectly several times, either by yourself and/or in front of a few colleagues.

At some point during the practice stage, you will surprise yourself with the confidence that you are ready. And yes, you are!

2. *Know your audience*

To make an effective presentation, you should be the subject matter expert or have close personal knowledge of the topic. You must prepare the presentation by knowing who the people in the audience are. How will they receive the content? And what delivery style will they enjoy the most? Do some basic research on the audience prior to the event to be fully confident in your content and delivery style. The quality and veracity of your presentation must equal the audience's interest and intellect. It is always a good idea to meet and mingle with the audience before the formal presentation begins. It will put you at ease, alleviate nervousness, and make the audience more accepting of your presentation. Do make eye contact with the people you just gotten to know and come close to them in the audience during your talk, if the setting is appropriate to do so.

3. *Speak with conviction*

You have created an exciting presentation, practiced many times, and built up the confidence to share your expertise with the audience! Now is the time to show your conviction about what you have to say. People will not only listen to the words but also enjoy your enthusiasm and feel your emotions. Deliver your words clearly and with high and low pitch or volume as appropriate. Monotone voice, low energy, and lack of enthusiasm in your sound of voice will be a turn off for the audience. On the other hand, people will enjoy and embrace the conviction in your style, confidence in your words, energy, enthusiasm, and emotions in your tone of voice!

4. *Follow the basics*

There are a lot of self-help programs and books for those preparing to give a presentation. Here are a few basics that, if followed, will separate you from the "speaking pack!"

> ➢ *Be sincere in your words.*
> ➢ *Be genuine in your emotions.*
> ➢ *Be enthusiastic in your style.*
> ➢ *Speak plainly and clearly.*
> ➢ *Keep good eye contact with entire group.*
> ➢ *If on stage, avoid being behind the lectern for too long.*
> ➢ *When near the audience, walk around and engage.*
> ➢ *Get to the point often and use high or low pitch.*
> ➢ *Be aware of your body language and facial expressions.*
> ➢ *If Microsoft PowerPoint is being used, keep text brief and images that are easy to comprehend.*
> ➢ *Offer to take questions at the end of the presentation.*
> ➢ *Do not take risk of opening with a joke. It may not work.*
> ➢ *You may share a brief personal story at the beginning to get the audience's attention.*

5. *Close powerfully.*

People in the audience are very likely to retain your message during the last two minutes of your presentation than at any other time. Wrapping up with your key points at the close is the best way to make some memorable moments for the audience. Like the bow on a present, make sure to tie all the ideas, messages, and takeaways together so the audience has one package to carry out of your presentation. Be very emphatic, use powerful words, and engage with genuine emotions to close the presentation. Thank the people in the audience, the organization who invited you, and the team of people who had put the event together. Everyone likes to clap for those that made it happen, and your presentation will end with the loud sound of applause!

Communication is the art of sharing thoughts and ideas among people. It is also a medium to send a message to another person or a group of people. Effective interpersonal communication requires certain skills. Some people have this ability naturally, and others learn it formally or through life experiences. The basic principles are the same. One must be an active, empathetic, respectful, and an engaged listener when interacting with others. You must be sincere, authentic, and respectful of others. When making a group presentation, one must articulate the message appropriately and sincerely and share with enthusiasm and conviction. The basic and simple principles noted above can help anyone be an effective communicator! They will enjoy the respect, trust, and attention of others when practicing these principles!

Questions to ponder about your interpersonal communication skills:

1. Do you pay undivided attention when listening to others?
2. Do you capture the words, the emotion, and the intent?
3. Do you repeat back to verify if what you understood is accurate?
4. Do you speak with a pleasant tone of voice?
5. Do you maintain a positive facial expression?
6. Do you speak clearly and with a smile even when on the phone?
7. Do you show your gratitude to the speaker and the listener as well?

Questions to ponder about your group presentation skills:

1. Do you prepare, practice, and not fear?
2. Do you develop ideas and concepts in your mind first?
3. Do you learn the audience and their veracity of knowledge?
4. Do you meet and mingle with the audience prior to your presentation?
5. Do you project genuine emotions and enthusiasm while speaking?
6. Do you speak plainly and clearly?

7.   Do you close powerfully with a few key messages?

If the answer to any of these pondering questions is a no, the leader needs to learn and practice these effective communication principles purposefully!

8

Continue to Learn and Grow

Leadership and learning are indispensable to each other.

—*John F. Kennedy, Thirty-Fifth US President*

Successful leaders have a "growth mindset." They want to continuously gain more knowledge, learn more skills, and develop additional strengths related to their job responsibilities. They have a passion for learning, and they acknowledge that the professional growth is a continuous process and it happens incrementally. As they grow, they also gain more energy and vigor so they can perform their jobs even better. They also realize that they must be out of their comfort zone to keep growing.

As successful leaders continue to improve their skills and capabilities, they also begin to positively impact their team and the organization. They set an example for their people and inspire them to do the same. They offer to invest in their people's growth, if people are willing to put forth the effort and the dedication that is needed. Great leaders simultaneously work on bringing a positive and impactful change in their personal life as well. They want to become better people and live a meaningful, exciting, and rewarding life.

*Passion is energy. Feel the power that comes
from focusing on what excites you.*

—*Oprah Winfrey, Famous Author and Television Personality*

In 1987, I was the general manager at a major corporate services account in the Dallas area for the management services company I was working for. I received many compliments from my superiors about how well this account was performing both operationally and financially. They also liked many new and innovative ideas we had implemented. I also knew that the client was very happy with the company and my team's performance.

At the yearend performance review, I was asked if there was any training or developmental course I wanted to take to further grow. I, of course, said, "Yes!" I wanted to take an English language linguistic course so that I can improve my pronunciation of certain words that I always had difficulty with. My leaders and the HR director agreed to pay for up to twelve one-on-one sessions with an English linguistics professor. I enjoyed this personalized course and was dedicated to improving my linguistics and pronunciations. *I learned, grew, and improved my spoken English language skills, which helped me in my overall communication skills! A year later, I was promoted to the district manager position.* This is just one example of my professional growth in my more than forty years career in the hospitality industry.

I also want to share a significant personal lifestyle improvement that I made to live a better and healthy life. I had started smoking in 1967 while in college. It was a cool thing to do. For many years, I never thought of any bad effects of smoking until one day in 1984. My four-year-old daughter and I were playing in the backyard of our house. After a while, I said I needed a cigarette break. Instantly with a firm voice she told me, "Dad, I don't like when you smoke."

Every parent can understand how her heartfelt words hit me like a ton of bricks. I immediately thought seriously to quit. I tried a few different methods but could not quite fully quit. I did cut back to only about a half pack a day, for the next many years, but still, I was not successful to fully quit.

Fast-forward to Saturday, September 4, 2004. Former president Bill Clinton had his heart surgery on that day. Around noontime, I turned on a cable news channel to just catch up on the news. There was a press conference going on by the four surgeons updating on the surgery they had just performed. They continued how the surgery was very successful and that the president was resting comfortably. When they started taking questions from the reporters, a female reporter asked, "How was Hillary and Chelsea doing?"

The lead surgeon said that they were "waiting patiently!"

At that time, I did not have a "Hillary" in my life, but I did have a "Chelsea." My daughter was now twenty-four, and I remembered what she had told me when she was four. I was hit with a ton of bricks again. This time, I had to fully quit. I did not want my daughter waiting patiently, if I was having a surgery because of any ailment from my smoking. *I had to quit, and I did! Instantly. I quit cold turkey!* I threw away a half pack of cigarettes, the ash tray, and the book of matches. It was 12:04 p.m., Central time, that day when this happened. I never touched a cigarette ever again! I did it for my daughter, but it benefitted me and my health. After thirty-seven years of smoking, I finally fully quit. Thank goodness, my doctors now tell me that my chest X-rays show that my lungs are clear. I made a personal improvement that I can share with happiness, smile, and in good health.

> *I learned to always take on things, I had never done before. Growth and comfort do not co-exist.*
>
> —*Ginny Rometty, Executive Chairman, IBM Corporation*

Even though success is defined differently by different people, but in all definitions, growth is one of the most common components. In the hospitality industry, different leaders may choose different growth and developmental paths as they feel what they need. They must also first enjoy the field or the profession that they are in to envision further growth. Here are eight most common and highly impactful attributes that can help leaders further fuel their growth as a leader.

1. *Personal vision*

The first step to achieving success and a lifetime of personal satisfaction is knowing what your natural talents and personality traits are. Career choices based on what you enjoy doing the most are very likely to bring you inner joy and pinnacle of success. It will also cultivate a passionate desire to continuously grow!

2. *Personal dedication*

Once you know what you want to become or achieve, it is crucial to make a personal commitment to prepare and plan for what is needed to reach your goals and dreams. The higher the goals, the more dedication is required. Personal sacrifices made during the growth phase generally have enormous rewards.

3. *High degree of emotional intelligence*

Through this journey of professional growth, everyone faces unplanned challenges, physical fatigue and, at times, emotional weakness. Your patience, calmness, hopes, and dreams, and your passion will keep you emotionally grounded and propel you moving forward. Some leaders have this ability and trait naturally. Others learn it in a purposeful manner.

4. *Technical knowledge*

Whatever your dreams or goals, it will very likely require a technical education whether a diploma, a four-year college degree, or a postgraduate education. Although many well-known and highly successful people had not even attended a college or finished college education. John D. Rockefeller, one of the wealthiest Americans of all time and founder of the Standard Oil Company, Inc.; and Dave

Thomas, founder of Wendy's, were not even high school graduates. Bill Gates, founder of the Microsoft Corporation, did not even finish college.

But for a vast majority of us, the road to success and growth and personal and professional life achievements is first receiving the best possible education. The more you dedicate to receiving great education, the higher the likelihood of achieving superior grades and other academic recognitions.

5. *Developed knowledge*

Once the formal education is complete, you will then need to learn and develop more practical and usable knowledge. This is even more significant for those who may not have reached their potential during college in receiving higher grades! You will need to take every opportunity to attend professional, career-related seminars, and subject matter conferences. You will also need to participate in special projects and new and innovative initiatives. To further develop your knowledge, you should also seek to learn other skills that will expand your expertise and help you further grow!

Innovation distinguishes between a leader and a follower.

—*Steve Jobs, Cofounder and Former CEO of Apple Inc.*

6. *Analytical skills*

Analytical skills have two components. Data analysis and decision-making. Understanding of the data requires attention to detail and clarity. Simplicity of reading and understanding data is more effective than overanalyzing. Making decisions based on data analysis requires a time-lapse thinking, and often, further clarity. You must be absolutely certain that the decisions being made will turn out to be the right decisions.

7. *Problem-solving skills*

Problem-solving skills have two components. Critical thinking and being flexible. Critical thinking skill prompts you to clearly understand the scope of the problem or an issue and identify the causes. Being flexible empowers you to find rational, practical, or even creative solutions. It may also tempt you to seek help when appropriate, to resolve any problem that you may be experiencing for the first time.

8. *Writing skills*

Writing skill is far more important than commonly understood. In today's business world, we write emails, hand notes, and other communication vehicles, e.g., marketing materials, business letters. A simple educational course on this skill is essential. Appropriately written emails, notes, etc. make a positive impact on the reader. On the other hand, poorly written emails can cause hidden misunderstandings. People often retain what they understood and choose not to clarify. There are also small books available to further improve your communication skills. I recommend the one I read, *Effective Communication Skills* by Marsha Ludden

Champions keep playing until they get it right.

—*Billie Jean King, Female Tennis Legend*

Questions to ponder about your desires to continue to learn and grow:

1. Do you have a personal vision for growth in your position?
2. Do you have a passion for innovation?
3. Do you dedicate part of your day to think, *What if?*
4. Do you handle stress fairly well?
5. Do you participate in activities or trainings that help you develop?

6.   Do you solve problems at work methodically?
7.   Do you write in a simple and clear manner?

If the answer to any of these pondering questions is a no, the leader needs to invest in their own growth and development plans.

9

Celebrate Your Team's Successes

Celebrate your success and find humor in your failures.

—Sam Walton, Founder of Walmart, Inc.

Celebration is an inherent part of American culture. We celebrate everything! From national holidays to personal events and from religious festivities to other key milestones. We are a nation of celebrations! We enjoy the great feeling, the fun, and the joy it brings to us! We feel excited, rejuvenated, and recharged! Celebrations bring us even closer to our family and friends. *We almost always celebrate like there is no tomorrow, and we love it!*

But then "tomorrow" comes. The excitement, the fun, and the joy from the celebration subsides, and now we must go back to work! Back to the daily routine, and for most of us, it takes a bit more effort to get going!

But wait! Imagine if the workplace had its own culture of celebrations! What if the organization and the leader you work with understood the value of celebrations? The excitement, the energy, and the great feeling it brings to you and the entire team. What if they knew how it motivates and recharges you to perform at a much higher level, and how it helps build great team spirit?

Successful leaders seize on every opportunity to celebrate their teams. They show their gratitude and acknowledge their team's successes through celebrations. They also understand the positive impact celebrations have on their employees' performance and their attitude. In the hospitality industry where people serve other people, a positive mindset and great attitude of well-celebrated employees is always noticed, respected, and appreciated by the patients, customers, and other end users. *These celebrated and motivated employees always look forward to "tomorrow" at work, and they love it!*

Here are nine ideas for creating a culture of celebrations in the hospitality industry where employees feel respected, appreciated, and celebrated as part of the organization's culture.

1. *New employees onboarding celebration*

Very often we celebrate when someone is leaving the organization. Why not celebrate when new employees join the team? At least once a month, plan a formal event to celebrate the arrival of new members of the team. Let everyone welcome them and get to know each other.

2. *Colleague milestones and personal accomplishments celebration*

Organizations should formally acknowledge and celebrate employees' personal achievements. This may include completing a certification course, earning a college degree while working, and even a close relative's educational accomplishments. Also celebrate employees' birthdays and work anniversaries. Such events build a long-term loyalty to the organization.

3. *New project launch celebration*

Every new project or a new product should be launched in an enthusiastic and well-celebrated manner. A formal launch celebration event will get the entire team excited. All details of the new venture should be shared, and the team who built the project should be acknowledged. Such events create a positive team energy toward achieving desired outcomes.

4. *Monthly progress updates celebration*

Leaders should keep the team updated regularly on the new projects and celebrate the progress being made along the journey to achieving the desired outcomes. A monthly formal celebration event should be planned for these updates. Such events recharge employees for even greater team efforts going forward.

5. *Bimonthly operational achievements celebration*

Employees want to know how well the organization is doing. They want to put forth all efforts for the organization to be successful and achieve desired outcomes. Leaders should keep everyone updated with the state of the organization. Successes should be celebrated, and challenges, if any, addressed. Such events keep the team moving forward.

6. *Quarterly star performers celebration*

Every team has star performers. Grateful leaders celebrate these employees to show their gratitude in a formal manner. Such celebrations should happen at least quarterly, and the entire organization should be invited. This gesture brings a positive energy to the entire team.

7. *Annual national recognition week celebration*

Annual nationally recognized employees' weeks such as environmental services employees' week should be well-planned and celebrated throughout the organization. The entire leadership team should appreciate and recognize hard work and dedication of all employees. This weeklong celebration reinvigorates the team.

8. *National and global holidays celebration*

National holidays such as Thanksgiving Day, Independence Day, as well as holidays recognized from other nationalities should also be celebrated at work. Organizations should integrate cultural celebrations of colleagues as they are celebrated in their native culture. This gesture helps build employees' loyalty to the organization and a greater bond among team members.

9. *Ongoing and on-the-spot celebration*

Employees should also be recognized and celebrated on an ongoing basis for personal achievements at work such as perfect attendance, etc. A formal employee recognition program should also be in place to congratulate employees who receive customer compliments. When an employee receives a compliment from a patient or a customer, they should be celebrated on the spot in some complimentary manner. Such programs motivate employees to go the extra mile for every customer.

> *Celebrate what you have accomplished, but raise the bar a little higher each time you succeed.*
>
> —Mia Hamm, American Soccer Player, Olympic and World Cup Champion

In the service industry, we need more celebrations. Organizations and leaders who celebrate their employees' contributions and successes, often and in a formal manner, reap great rewards! They are committed to showing their gratitude to the employees in a meaningful and celebratory manner on an ongoing basis. They know how celebrations positively impact on employees' morale, energy, and dedication. When employees see and feel how well they are appreciated and celebrated, they look forward to going to work every "tomorrow!"

Questions to ponder about how you celebrate team's successes:

1. Do you celebrate new team members joining your team?
2. Do you celebrate team member's personal accomplishments?
3. Do you create a celebration event when a new product or service is launched?
4. Do you celebrate your team members in your monthly team meeting?
5. Do you celebrate the team's collective achievements regularly?
6. Do you surprise team members with on-the-spot celebration?
7. Do you formally celebrate national team's recognition days such as national foodservice workers week or national administrative professionals day?

If the answer to any of these questions is a no, the leaders should reconsider building a culture of appreciating and celebrating team contributions to the organization.

Notes and Quotes of My Colleagues

Over the years, throughout my career, I have worked with many admirable colleagues who had impeccable leadership qualities. Also, for the past six years, I have worked with other support services consultants who have had a lifetime of accomplished leadership experiences. I thought that it would add value to this book by adding their one or two key principles that they followed over their professional careers. These are all accomplished people in the hospitality services industry, and their comments are very relevant.

Work with people, your team is your people.

Responsibility and authority have to be balanced.

—Michael Salvatore, CEC Senior Director,
Ruck-Shockey Associates

Never ask an associate to do something, that you wouldn't do.

Honesty is the best policy because you can never remember the lies.

—Joe Morgan, District Manager (Retired),
Marriott Management Services

Accountability starts with you.

Encourage people to share their knowledge and expertise.

—Anita Zefo, RD Consultant, Ruck-Shockey Associates

Give more than you take, it makes a big positive impact on the team/organization.

Do more than you have to, it helps you become better and grow.

—Julie Jones, MS RD Consultant, Ruck-Shockey Associates

Meet people where they are.

Practice Excellence without arrogance.

—Charissa Gray, People Ambassador, Certified MBTI Facilitator

Work together to achieve more.

Lead by example.

—Deb Pogodzinski, MPH RDN

Never be afraid to set higher goals than people think, can be achieved.

Be on the floors to see what and how team members are doing.

—Edward Acevedo, Director of Environmental Services

Leadership is both a responsibility and a privilege.

Seek responsibility and take responsibility for your actions.

—Dexter Hancock, MS RD Senior Consultant, Ruck-Shockey Associates

If you want to climb the ladder, help the person above you to reach higher level.

If you don't have fun at work, why would you go to work.

—Jimmy Fetters, Director of Operations

Being present and listening to what others have to say is very important.

Leading by example.

—Jennifer Day, Administrative Specialist, Patient Care Services

Set clear expectations.

Celebrate successes.

—Cynthia Marshall, Associate Partner at Curative

Provide clear communication, feedback and encouragement.

Help people grow and develop.

—Robert Hofacre, Senior Consultant, Ruck-Shockey Associates

Maintain business relationships, centered around Trust.

—Cathy Wedman, MS RD Client Executive, Sodexo Healthcare

Overcoming adversity and failure is the key to leadership.

—Bernie King, Client Executive, Sodexo Corporate Services

Greet people coming to work every morning.

Listen to people with a smile and intent to learn.

—John Hines, Career Coach, Collin College Workforce Programs

About the Author

Khalid Shiekh has served in leadership positions with two of the world's most successful hospitality services companies for more than thirty-six years, from corporate food services district manager to health care support services senior director in major medical centers around the United States. In his fortunate journey in many mid-level leadership positions throughout his career, he earned many performance awards, leadership recognitions, and mentoring and coaching honors, for which the author is forever grateful to the teams and the organizations.

Khalid Shiekh, Principal
Khalid Shiekh LLC
Las Vegas, Nevada. USA 89183

CPSIA information can be obtained
at www.ICGtesting.com
Printed in the USA
BVHW071241130423
662286BV00007B/490